MORE

CATHERINE AUMAN

"For those readers, men and women, who wish to enrich their love lives, investigating Catherine's sage and well-considered advice could be just the answer and the path you're looking for!"

— *Osho Times*, international online magazine

"For many years there have been books about how to be tricky, guarded, or false in the world of dating by "the rules." Thank goodness that Catherine Auman has spelled out a different and better way. This is a book for people who want integrity, authenticity, and genuine connection to truly happen. It's a much-needed approach that feels both new and timeless."

— Leonard Felder, PhD, author of
Fitting in is Overrated

"I love this book. Thank you, Catherine Auman. If you haven't read or don't know anything about the tantric approach to dating, check out this book and consider attending one of Catherine's workshops—truly game changing."

— Carina Eriksson, Professional Matchmaker

"The book *Tantric Dating* offers much-needed clarity and insight into the world of sacred sexuality and the much-bantered term "tantra". The author is the real deal and she teaches that love is always available and changing our perception is an important place to begin."

— Corey Folsom, Sex & Relationship Coach

"When it comes to dating coaching, I would completely trust Catherine Auman and welcome her perspective."

— Vince Kelvin, Seminar Leader and Coach

Tantric Dating

Bringing Love
and Awareness
to the Dating Process

Catherine Auman, LMFT

Green Tara Press

Green Tara Press

Los Angeles, CA

www.greentarapress.com

© 2017, 2020 Catherine Auman

All Rights Reserved. First edition 2017.

Second edition 2020.

Library of Congress Control Number: 2020910065

Library of Congress In-Publication Data

Auman, Catherine I.

Tantric Dating: Bringing Love and Awareness to the Dating Process

1. Self Help 2. Dating 3. Spiritual

ISBN 978-1-945085-06-2 Paperback

ISBN 978-1-945085-05-5 Electronic Book Text

Author Photo by Charity Burnett

Cover and interior book design by Lilly Penhall

CONTENTS

INTRODUCTION

It was a major birthday—one of those years when you take stock of if you're where you want to be. In most areas of life, I had to admit I was doing great: successful in my chosen career, great health, lovely friends, a cute apartment, financially stable—most of the things that everyone wants—except for the only thing that had ever really mattered—being in a soulmate relationship with my Perfect Beloved.

Not that I hadn't tried. Ever since I first discovered boys (outside my brother) in kindergarten, I'd been trying. After countless blind dates, bad dates and bad boys, relationship advice books and columns, online and in-person dating, an early foray (a bit unwillingly) into "free love" culture, endless hours of therapy, many, many relationships and two failed marriages, I had to admit: I was a Dating Disaster.

I recounted all this to a long-time friend in the Bay Area who asked how she could support me. Since she was actively involved in online dating, I suggested we cheerlead each other a couple times a week. We began chatting frequently late at night, reviewing dates and deciphering texts. Then she promptly met someone and with that, I was alone again.

I made the decision to go for it. Really go for it this time, no matter what. I was going to get to the bottom of this and become a Master of Dating and Relationships. I decided to hack dating once and for all, whatever it took. And for me, it took a lot.

Sitting on my couch on Saturday nights, watching Netflix while sipping a glass of wine wasn't working. I needed to get into action. I joined five online dating sites and over twenty Meetups (which is great because you are always getting invitations in your inbox). I downloaded an app which had a calendar of all the art openings in town and ventured out to art gallery openings (free wine and intriguing hipsters). I went back to therapy to complete some still-unfinished business from childhood (I had been in therapy a lot, but still … sometimes when you come from a difficult childhood it takes a while), and hired a coach. An unusual dating coach—I hired a Pickup Artist.

I had read *The Game* back in the 00s and realized those guys know a lot that is not taught in "girl game" (dating) books which overall are pretty lame. I'd always been a bit shy and afraid to go up and speak to a man I found attractive, and pickup coaching got me over all that.

With the help of my coach I began going out "in the field," meaning into real life where men might be hanging out. I went to anything I could think of to meet men, mostly dead ends. Little by little my dating skills improved, and the men I was attracting grew closer and closer to my heart's longing. Dating actually became fun, and I played in the field enjoying my new freedom.

I went on over 150 online first dates, followed by second and third dates, and sometimes it seemed to be working out. I met 2-3 men a week, sometimes 2-3 in a day. I made myself go out: Meetups, gallery openings, singles events, networking events, Green Drinks, poetry readings, museum outings, and basically every time I went to Trader Joe's. I traveled with wing-girls and without and challenged myself to approach men I found interesting. I created little games for when I was discouraged (which was often), such as before I went to sleep, I needed to contact 10 guys online. Usually 2 would get back. I made progress in therapy, and worked hard with my coach.

One question always nagged me though, how did all of this coexist with my spiritual life?

You see, I'd lived at the Osho ashram in India for a year, a full-time immersion in tantra and meditation. The way potential lovers met there was very different than in the conventional world. People there were friends first, and after that would see if a sexual friendship was possible. In our contemporary dating scene in the West, "the friend zone" is considered death. At the ashram, and in tantra, the Friend Zone is exactly where you want to be. Only if you and your lover are friends will you establish the trust and intimacy necessary for good sex and a good relationship to happen.

In exercises in the tantra groups, we got close to and "fell in love" with people we would never have chosen if we had let our eyes be the primary criteria the way we do in the West. We learned to feel another person's frequency, to assess our level of comfort and safety. We practiced telling the radical truth to each other, a practice frowned on by conventional dating. We enjoyed the process of meeting one another rather than considering it a huge, irritating chore. And we experienced loving who was present in this moment, rather than waiting for one who may never come.

For years, I couldn't reconcile what I'd learned at the ashram with the conventional dating world I was now attempting to navigate. But little by little, I began to put together how dating could be part of the spiritual path. I watched my judgments, my prejudices—did I really believe that only conventionally good-looking people were worthy of love? I observed how I searched for the wrong things instead of the only quality that's really important—kindness.

I came to realize that the reason I had attracted men who were half-loving was because I was half-loving. I painfully accepted that the common denominator in my relationship problems was me. And if I wanted to meet a man who was truly loving, I would have to evolve beyond being unloving toward the men I was meeting or even viewing online.

I had to confront the romantic Disney-esque fantasies that had been fed to me in movies, books, and songs that love would come to me by magic. I had to stand up to the ageism of the culture and inside myself that women (people) of a certain age are too old to find love, or that men only like younger women. This is emphatically not true. After I had made progress in my dating work, I dated men from ages 28 to 68 and everywhere in between. (The 28-year old, a true looker from Turkey, begged me to take him as my boyfriend. I said no.) I had to work hard to overcome all these cultural myths. Because they are myths and because they're commonly held to be true, they are insidious.

Eventually I became more loving through my process of "Tantric Dating," loving enough to attract a loving man. After 3 ½ years of hard effort, I met my Perfect Beloved. I didn't recognize him at first. It's true he pursued me, but if I hadn't learned what I did through decades of work on myself, we would not have met nor have the Perfect Soulmate relationship we have today. We got married after two years of being together, and together have created a relationship where both of us are always saying, "I didn't know a relationship could be this good."

And so, I want to teach you my method of Tantric Dating that attracted and created the relationship I dreamed of since kindergarten. Some people have reported profound shifts in their attitudes after reading this book. Others have criticized it for being a little slim, which it is. I still stand by its content because if you really digest it, it's all you'll need. Please bring the willingness to examine the brainwashing of the conventional world and decide for yourself. Choose to become the loving person that your heart knows you are. Share it with the world, and Love cannot deny you.

TANTRIC DATING MINDSET

What Do We Mean by "Tantra?"

When most people hear the word "tantra" they think of sex, and often here in the Western world you'll see "tantra" used as a marketing term such as come to this or buy this because it's TANTRA, you've seen this right? Actually, Osho, a spiritual teacher and Tantra Master from India, explained it this way: At the essence, all teachings basically boil down to one of two paths to God, enlightenment, realization, whatever term you want to use: the Yogic or the Tantric.

In New Age circles you'll see it all mushed together, but if you look closely, you'll see that there are actually two separate paths. The Yogic path says that there's something you have to do to get to God: you have to eat a certain way, or you have to never be angry, you have to wear a certain kind of clothes, or you should not have sex. There are a myriad of ways you can develop and try to change yourself, and in the West we would say we're very "yogic" because we're all developing ourselves, we want to become better, we want to become superior people, and we want to become high(er).

The Tantric path, which is not as well-known, is that there's nothing to be done, everything is already perfect. In this moment, is anything missing? All is permitted, all is holy, all is divine, there's nothing you need to improve. You don't need to eat a certain way; you don't need to stop being sexual; if you're angry be angry. Osho would have people get totally angry, and in his Dynamic Meditation they'd just go crazy and mad and spill out all their anger instead of trying to repress it. The point was not to create a world full of angry people, the point was to create people who are fully human, and being angry is an essential part of being human. So the tantric path would say that everything about you is human and beautiful including your anger, including your pain, including your sexuality. Osho said celebrate everything you are: this is the tantric path.

There have been different paths calling themselves tantra, and you will find some that actually are yogic in that they teach exercises to become a super lover, a tantra superstar. Osho's Neo-Tantra was not about that; it was facing your fears, growing yourself up about love and sex, and in the process experiencing yourself as a fully sexual being.

Tantric Dating Vs. Conventional Dating

Conventional dating in and of itself encourages us to think there's something wrong with other people and something wrong with us. Other people don't look right, and you don't look right. They're not lovable, and you're not lovable. They don't have the cool moves; you don't have the cool moves. The conventional mindset encourages us to see other people and ourselves as weird and unattractive and disposable.

The conventional dating process encourages us to feel I'm not doing it right, I don't meet the right people, I'm not attractive enough to date. For women it's "I'm not pretty enough" and for guys it's "I'm not accomplished enough" continuing the deadly cycle of over-focus on women's appearance and men's financial status. These myths about who's lovable and who isn't actually keep people home and not looking for love because they believe the myth that "I'm not good enough;" "I'm not pretty enough;" "I'm not accomplished enough;" "I'm not hot enough;" it's endless. It's all ego stuff that someone's surface appearance is not to my liking.

Everyone you meet on a date is seen through the frame of whether they are a candidate for the fantasy of perfect love or not. This is very harsh isn't it? If they're not a candidate, get rid of them quickly followed by an amusing story for friends: "God I couldn't stand being on that date for so long; it was so awful… etc." This whole conventional mindset is anti-love, whether love for self or others.

From a tantric perspective every single person you meet is the right person in this moment. If you look at the person next to you, in this moment this is your beloved. She or he is your true love, right here, right now. The beloved is not somebody you're going to meet in the future; it's not somebody who's going to ride in on a white horse or be spotted across the dance floor. Right now, this is where love is available; this is who it is possible to love. Are you available for this love?

If we're always thinking I can't love this other person because they aren't good enough for me that's about you, not the other person. How about: let me enjoy this other spiritual being and even if it's not the romantic fantasy, we are in this perfect spot together sharing love in this perfect moment.

Society is Against Love

Society is designed to lure you away from being intimate with others because you are not spending any money during this time. Intimacy is the enemy of consumerism because your sense of wellbeing is so greatly enhanced that you do not need to buy material goods to be happy.

—Peter Rengel

I first met Peter Rengel as one of the facilitators of the Love, Intimacy and Sexuality workshops at the Human Awareness Institute (HAI). They're located in the Bay Area, and I learned a great deal while moving up to Level Five in their system. I also worked individually with Peter as my therapist, so I was lucky enough to learn a lot from this man whose life mission is "to help people love themselves more." How awesome is that?

Peter pointed out, as in the quote above, that society is designed to seduce you away from being intimate with others because you won't spend money if you're in love and satisfied. If you're in love and fulfilled, what do you need to buy?

I checked this out with a friend of mine who's been married for 25 years. He said oh yeah, he and his wife just work, stay in and cook, watch movies and make love, and that's about all they do. They are very happy with their lives.

Think how much money is spent in the dating process; it's a whole industry. You have to spend money on your dates, buy expensive food, and drink more alcohol than you usually drink. You have to buy dating clothes, which for women must be sexy. Guys have to show off how much money they make. Certain restaurants position themselves as dating hot spots as well as certain hip bars, and there are pricey singles' events and online dating sites to join. It's a multi-million dollar business to keep you single and unhappy because if you fall in love and fall out of all that and therefore aren't spending any money, society will stop. So the whole shebang is anti-love, as Peter pointed out, which is really mind boggling.

You'll also notice it's no accident that the conventional dating mindset is the consumer model in which you are looking to acquire a high-value item, and then when that one is used up you purchase another that is presumably more "expensive."

The Appearance Issue

For many people the biggest barrier to finding a partner is the appearance of the other person. It's hard to live in this culture and not be brainwashed to believe that only certain people are attractive. In the mainstream mindset, only conventionally good-looking people get to be considered sexually appealing and therefore worthy of love.

I was lucky enough to have this pseudo-reality shattered in tantra groups and later on at HAI. The first method used to challenge us was having us be naked all the time. It's difficult at first, but you get used to being around what people really look like which is quite different of course than the photoshopped images we are taught to lust after. It's a good practice to get comfortable being naked with other people (which you can do at spas or clothing-optional resorts)—you get to witness everyone's vulnerable humanity.

What took it to another level of awareness for me, though, was the exercises we did naked and blindfolded where we would reach out and touch and stroke each other—maybe an arm, someone's precious heart—and we would sense without being able to see: what is the nature of my attraction to this person? What kind of energy do the two of us have without the prejudice of sight? We would move on to touch somebody else asking ourselves, what is the actual nature of my attraction with this body? Is it a friendship? A sexual connection? A combination of that? Is it repellent because it reminds me of my parents? Or a soft, being, togetherness?

Not being able to see honed my ability to sense the differences in energies and the truth of my attraction. Those of us in the group found that we were attracted to people we never would have imagined, and we all fell in love with each other no matter what we looked like.

Looks are one thing we can't control, along with age and bone structure. For me it's actually become one of the least interesting things about a person, because it's what people are born with and can't control. I would much prefer to feel the actual nature of my attraction to a person versus what I've been conditioned to desire. We've been conditioned to eat junk food; we've been conditioned to want many things that are "toxic." It's the ego clinging to the idea that I, the great I, must have a person on my arm who makes me look even better.

The Whole Issue of "Chemistry" and "Trusting Your Gut"

In the dating world, most everyone nods and agrees when people say that what they're looking for is "chemistry." Other similar phrases you'll hear are "using their intuition" and "trusting their gut." These are often the same people who believe they can tell within five seconds whether or not someone is worthy of their love.

I'd like to address that as a therapist. An article in my book, *Shortcuts to Mindfulness: 100 Ways to Personal and Spiritual Growth* entitled "Your Worst Nightmare," cites Terry Gorski, a renowned chemical dependency counselor. Gorski states that when you have the feeling of love at first sight, you should turn around and run in the opposite direction. Sometimes what we think of as "chemistry" means programming from our childhood, and it may not be a good sign.

As an extreme example, we've all heard of a woman beaten by her father in childhood, who now doesn't leave relationships where the man beats her up. We wonder, why doesn't she leave? Well, she was programmed in childhood that love equals getting beat up, so she's going to feel "chemistry" when she meets a guy who carries that energy. At first he's going to seem like a gentleman, and she's going to think, "Oh, finally I met somebody who isn't an abuser," but that "chemistry" that comes from wiring in childhood is going to prevail most of the time unless she's done work to disempower it.

So when people say they're looking for "chemistry" often they are looking at issues that are going to trigger unfinished business from the past. Hopefully that will entice the person to get into therapy and stop being attracted to someone who hurts them or is in some other way unkind or not good for them.

There are many things that can trigger a strong reaction to meeting a new person. It's possible the feeling is a good sign, but I'm suggesting that people not blindly go "Oh, it's chemistry." When you have that feeling, realize there could be many possibilities and don't just blindly believe it means this is "The One."

Is It Really Rejection?

Sophisticated conventional daters will sooner or later come across the mindset that "dating is a series of rejections" and that to be successful dater, it's about becoming okay with the inevitable. One aphorism you'll hear is "If you want to get more comfortable with rejection, go out and get rejected five times"—the idea being that you will learn to stop taking it so personally. In a way, I applaud these efforts as a step on the way to realizing that dating doesn't have to hurt so much, having gone through a similar process earlier myself. I remember a time when I was afraid to date because it seemed so awful to have to reject people, and I often hear women saying the same thing. Having to reject can be almost as painful as being the rejected one.

Some conventional daters use a phrase they've learned in 12-step programs that "Rejection is God's protection," helping them see that perhaps this was not the right person or the right time and that maybe the "rejection" happened for a good reason.

But what happens to us when we use this word "rejection?" What does "rejection" feel like? Terrible, bad, and humiliating. It also feels horrible and cruel to "reject" another human being. We must be careful in the way we choose our words—they can create all kinds of states, situations, and mindsets, and the word "rejection" can create incapacitating feelings.

What if we do away altogether with this concept of "rejection?" Instead, we could see dating situations as we do with potential friends: you meet someone at an event and hang out; you have a good time talking, but you aren't necessarily moved to make plans to see them again. In dating, this would be called "rejection," but in ordinary life there's no rejecting going on, you just aren't going to hang out. In dating this scenario is experienced as painful, and it doesn't have to be any more so than it is meeting someone at a networking event.

What if we said instead "it's just not a good fit" or "s/he wasn't my cup of tea," or "seemed like a lovely person, but there must have been things I wasn't seeing about him/her." How about if we say if we're "ghosted:" "My goodness, that's a person who doesn't seem to communicate very well, because they seemed like they did but then suddenly they dropped off the planet. I need to be with a better communicator."

In using words the conventional dating mindset encourages us to use we may become tougher, steeling ourselves against "rejection." The whole concept of "rejecting" comes from the ego: this person is not good enough for me, or I am not good enough for them. What if we just enjoy our precious time with this person, and if it's not right to be with them again, it doesn't have to hurt us. It could be held in a loving way that's neither rejecting people nor being rejected by them.

What About Toxic People?

I know it's quite popular, but I don't agree with this concept that certain people are toxic. It doesn't make any sense to me at all to label people that way; I find it harsh and inaccurate. Perhaps it might be helpful to label some behaviors that people do as "toxic" so that we learn to develop strong boundaries, but the appointing of some beings as "toxic" is often used as a justification not to love people.

In a tantric perspective nothing is toxic; in a yogic perspective everything is either toxic or non-toxic. In the tantric worldview nothing is forbidden; everything is holy. Therefore, a challenging relationship with a difficult person may be just what we need to make us aware of where and how we need to grow.

Observe it: your mind is busy coming up with reasons why not to love people. They're toxic, or not good-looking enough, or not spiritual, or they have too many problems. Where are these people who have no problems? People come with problems, and they're going to stir you and make your life difficult, and that's a good thing.

This idea of "people who are toxic" could be a pretext for "how do I keep people away?" Not consciously, of course, it's subtle. Who can I keep away from me because they're too toxic, and they'll bring me problems? All of these people that I don't want to let close. Really, that's focusing on how to keep love away.

I'm asking you to flip your question 180 degrees to: How can I allow people to come close? Use your intelligence to figure out how to let people in instead of how to keep people out. Who are you going to allow yourself to love? Consider that instead of thinking about what and who is toxic. Open up and let us in.

We're All Spiritual Brothers and Sisters Helping Each Other Grow

An attitude I developed while hanging out at the Ashram and basking in the tantric atmosphere was *we're all spiritual brothers and sisters helping each other grow*. I'd never thought of the men I was involved with this way, so it was revolutionary, and I'd never been in an environment where men and women treated each other as such. It was beautiful and loving in stark contrast to conventional dating where everyone considers others as either a candidate for the Perfect Love or the garbage can.

A brother of mine on the planet, a spiritual brother or sister who's also evolving—I believe that everyone's evolving even if they don't use that language. We come together for these romantic and sexual encounters to evolve in a certain way together. We don't know for how long; we're not in charge of that part, I don't think. So it's been a helpful mindset for me to hold that we're helping each other grow, rather than clinging to a fantasy outcome that might or might not be for our higher good.

The fairy-tale fantasy is that a man is going to come fully formed as the Perfect Prince, or for guys, that the Dream Woman is going to come as this totally voluptuous, always wanting to have sex, always loving person. If the Prince was always ready for sex that would be fine too, but it's this idea that these perfect lovers are going to come to us fully formed that's the cause of a lot of problems. Who's fully formed? Only a person who's not human or who's stopped growing, so when you meet a real person and they're not fully formed, you're going to be disappointed if you're immersed in the conventional mindset.

But if you're holding it that we're all evolving and growing and we're spiritual brothers and sisters, you can allow the other person to relax in your tender and warm presence and evolve along with you. Both men and women have difficult things to overcome as we are learning to become more loving, and this path of dating, relationships, and sexuality can be one of the roadways to God. It can rapidly accelerate your growth and lead you further along the path to becoming an ultimately loving person.

Blaming Other People for Why We're Not Loving

When we explain that the reason we don't have love in our lives is that we can't find the right person, or that other people are flawed or wrong in some way, it's putting the blame outside ourselves for why we don't have love, versus I'm not living in love because I'm not loving. The truth is: I'm not loving to the people I meet, I reject them, and I don't make time for them.

Some of the ancient *tantrikas* (people who practice tantra) were tortured for their beliefs because people were so prejudiced against them. In one sect, the couple lived their entire lives sewn together into one garment. Now think about it, in today's world you can barely stand to have your lover over for an hour and a half before you start bumping against something vaguely irritating.

Of course I'm exaggerating (am I?) but we've all gotten used to having things our own way, and our egos clash when we spend much time together. In one of the exercises at the ashram, we experimented with a partner where we didn't let go of their hand for three hours. We would walk around doing every minute thing together, and I saw how much time it takes to be intimate. It took so long to just reach out and get food in the food line, to walk over to the table together—it was exquisite and, you know, a real luxury. I really got the sense that it takes so much time to be loving, and we just don't have or make that time. Everyone's too busy.

If you want to sit and have a coffee date with some-one and you want to enjoy them no matter what they're like, you're going to have to relax and have it take time instead of be wondering how quickly you can leave. It's going to take time to figure out how to savor the person. It's going to take time to have love, and it's going to take time to turn yourself into a loving person.

I hear this a lot: I can't find anybody; there's nobody to love. Really? There are 10 million people in greater LA, 20 million in Southern California—how could you possibly not find someone? That's about you, that's about me, that's about us if we can't find someone; it's not about the lack of other candidates. If we're willing to take spiritual responsibility, it's not the other person's fault. The other person is an opportunity for us to learn to become more loving, and who does that need to be? That could be anyone—it could be that homeless person sitting on the bench, but we make it so hard.

It's Up to Me Whether I Love You or Not; It's Not Up to You

It's all up to me if I love you or not; it's not up to you. It actually has nothing to do with you whatsoever. It has everything to do with whether my heart's open to love or not. So when I'm sitting across from you at a coffee date and we're meeting for the first time or the tenth time, it's not about whatever characteristics and traits you may or may not have. I decide to love or not love. Not you.

It's a great spiritual exercise to sit and watch your ego try to convince you why it's not possible to love this person. Your ego will say, "well, she's wearing a watch like that—we can't love a person who wears that brand." That's me and not the watch-wearer, right? The type of watch she's wearing and whether that makes her loveable to me has nothing to do with her—it has to do with my prejudices. You can also use it if you're brave to show you how unloving you are, because your fantasy is that you're this great loving person, and you can't even love a simple being who's sitting across from you.

Watching oneself this way on dates can be used as a spiritual discipline to see "what in me is the way of love," because if I'm not meeting anybody through the dating process, it's about me, not the supposedly-deficient other people. If I have too many criteria about who I might deign to love I'll remain alone and lonely, because I have the mistaken belief that nobody—except my daydream lover—is good enough for me.

We can develop within ourselves a tantric approach that there are many ways to love "you," the "you" who is in front of me in this moment. In this moment I really can't think of any reason why not to love you. I don't know how long we're going to know each other—maybe for twenty more minutes and maybe two years and maybe the rest of our lives, but right now in this moment it's up to me, so I choose love.

The Invention of Romantic Love

I read a fascinating book in college called *Love in the Western World* that said that romantic love was invented in the 1200s by the Troubadours. You remember the Troubadours, wearing those sexy little puff pants, walking around playing lutes, singing about their ladylove. They would elevate a woman onto a pedestal and long ceaselessly for her; the whole point of chivalrous love was that it was never consummated. It was a sexist day and age, so it was all about men adoring a woman, and the point was to idealize the beloved but never come down to earth for love's trials and tribulations.

What's really fascinating, even more than the fact

that romantic love didn't exist before that time, was that the people who inspired it, the Cathars, were actually singing to God, not a woman. They were an ecstatic *bhakti* sort of cult, singing hymns to God in an almost sexual frenzy. They were persecuted for their beliefs and mode of worship (they were later burned alive) so they hid their passion by pretending their songs were about a woman instead of God.

So the whole notion of romantic love was a lie. It was a cover up for a yearning that is spiritual, not a desire for a human person. It was created to point towards something that's actually not achievable on the physical plane. Romantic love wasn't intended to result in what we would today consider a relationship. Instead it was about pining—the essence of romantic love is that you're in pain longing for a perfect person who doesn't exist and you can't have.

We celebrate romantic love; we want romantic love; I personally love the fantasy of romantic love. Everybody has had moments of perfect romantic love, right? And how long did they last? Hours, days, you can do it for years if the person is not available. If the person has rejected you, you can fantasize about them for decades. It was never meant to be anything tangible, or of the real world.

Osho once said that all your romantic love affairs will be thwarted so that you'll keep searching for what you're really seeking. Divine Love.

The Pain of Romantic Love is Good for You (To a Point)

Romantic love, as we said, as invented by the Troubadours, is a spiritual longing for what cannot be had here on the earth plane. The object of romantic love is not really a human being, it's an idealized image, perhaps a fragmented memory of a person we once knew. Romantic love actually prefers to be unrequited; causing a desire for someone you can't have that's so bad you want to tear your heart out. You elevate the other onto a pedestal above you, and thus you are of lesser value. To really make it passionate, it helps to have been rejected. If you imagine it was because you are not good enough or deficient in some way, well, that leads to some really delicious self-flagellation.

Could there be a spiritual purpose for this? How could it be good for us? I think it's explained by this Kahlil Gibran quote, "Your pain is the breaking of the shell that encloses your understanding." This has helped me understand why I've had pain; why my patients have pain, and why the human race suffers so much: because when we are in pain it breaks our hearts and that gives us an opportunity for understanding. We can begin to develop compassion for our own suffering and the suffering of others. Then Love starts becoming available, not as a fantasy "my lover looks like Brad Pitt" or some dream girl, but because I'm becoming a loving person to my neighbours, friends, family, and loved ones. I can start looking for someone who will love me back instead of rejecting me and finding me unworthy, leaving me feeling like pond scum.

A tantra teacher I met the other day said to me,

"The heart that breaks is not the True Heart." Wow! The True Heart isn't the egoic heart. Our limited little hearts break because we were looking for the wrong thing. We were looking for the fantasy Brad Pitt who is wealthy and fit and always does the right romantic things and drives such-and-such car and is my armpiece, impressing my friends. My ego can get all puffed up that I'm this great lover, when actually I'm not very loving at all because what I'm seeking is something to enhance my ego. That's what gets broken so we can actually become lovers.

The egoic mindset is, in order for me to be loving, the other person has to be what my ego wants them to be. I will only be loving if the other person is cool enough for me. I will only be loving if the other person is conventionally beautiful, or isn't of a different body size, or isn't an Arab or Muslim or Syrian or Jew or black or white, etc.—that's the only way I'll be loving. That's what's going on on the planet: You have to be a certain way for me to love you.

I'm Going to
Live in Love

Taking a stand that "I'm going to live in love" is say-ing I'm going to do this. I'm sure in your dating life you've come to a place where after a disappointment you decided to stop. I stopped for many years—I didn't believe it was possible to live in love. I came to realize that unless we have a strong intention that "I'm going to live in love," we're likely to give up.

I hear a lot of people say they'd be happy to find love "if it happens." "If it happens" is not going to happen. I had to make a concerted effort as I would for my career. If you're over 30 the love you're looking for is not going to happen magically. As one of my students reports, she met the love of her life "magically" after working on herself diligently for ten years. Being "in love" is a decision, it's not something that might or might not happen in a fairy land in the sky.

The law of attraction stuff out there that says that if we're radiating right it will show up—there's a certain truth to that, but not in the way people think. The first thing is to get really clear that you're going to live in love, and then you're going to need to make an action plan. How are you going to meet someone? It doesn't work to just leave it to chance. Look inside and ask yourself if you feel you're doing enough. I certainly didn't want to go on 150 first dates but that's what it took. Are you willing to put in the effort? Where are you going to put yourself in front of a person so that you can "magically" meet them?

Conventional dating advice is don't date unless this might be The One. Consequently, we're sitting home watching Netflix. If we start exercising the ability to open our hearts to people even if they're not The One, we get a lot closer to attracting our Beloved because we are starting to vibrate with the frequency of love. It starts with saying I don't want to be alone—I'm going to live in love, even before I meet The One.

How Do I Open More to Love?

The question comes up: "How do I open more to love?" If I'm working on myself to become a more loving person, and seeking increased emotional and sexual pleasure, how do I go about it?

I would offer you a beautiful, mind-blowing perspective from one of my teachers, Radha Luglio, who has a large tantra practice in Italy. When asked this question she answered: it's not a question of how do I open more, it's a question of where am I holding.

Wow. In this moment, if I pay attention, I can tell where I'm holding. And I've yet to meet a person who when asked where they're holding, isn't able to identify it immediately. Is it a tightness in the belly, the throat? Is there a restriction around the heart, the breath, the genitals? Is it a stuckness from a previous relationship that needs to be cleared? Perhaps a hardness around the heart, or a wish to slow down.

It's right here in the present moment. We can go in and do some deep work in psychotherapy which definitely helps, but in this moment where am I holding against love? You can ask this while in the moment with these people right now; you can ask it on a dinner date. My emotions seem to be freezing up; does this remind me of my mother? Or I don't like people like this, or am I just scared?

You can scan yourself while making love: where am I holding, where am I tensing up? How am I guarding myself against love in this moment? What am I telling myself; what is my mind saying? A lot of times when we're making love we get scared to go a little further, right? It's frightening to get more intimate, but that's about me; it's not the other person's fault. I'm not more loving because he's not making love right—we may try to make it their fault unless we can be strong and truthful and ask ourselves, how am I holding back at this moment from love and pleasure?

We're always trying to blame someone outside ourselves as to why we're not loving. It helps to actually go into the body and feel where the holding pattern is, and identify it. Awareness changes things. The very fact that you have taken responsibility for your own love and pleasure rather than blaming someone or something outside yourself changes the whole experience. Then you can breathe more fully into the present moment, face your fears, communicate, and expand into areas of yet-unknown bliss.

Advocating for Love

So what we are advocating is taking a look at how the conventional view of love actually destroys love, and then making the efforts necessary to turn ourselves into lovers, that is, truly loving people. Making a decision to go against the conventional worldview of daters-as-consumers deciding which shiny new object to purchase. Choosing against being people whose minds instead of hearts run the show, analyzing who is or is not worthy of love based on a set of prejudices as insidious as racism or religious intolerance.

In the world today we have a hate problem; and according to the World Health Organization, we have a growing loneliness and isolation problem which is as detrimental to health as smoking and heart disease. There are a lot of single people sitting in their homes feeling hopeless and lonely—they can't find love in a city of ten million people. It doesn't make sense. The problem is not that there's no one out there to love. The problem is that we're not loving enough to be able to see the abundance of potential lovers.

One way it makes sense is if I work on myself to become a loving person, I'll have ten million lovers. If there's ten million persons in the city, I have potentially ten million lovers—that's kind of sexy, isn't it?

When we are overflowing with love we love everything. You know those moments you've had when you love everything and everyone? Those times often don't last very long, but by working on yourself you can maintain them for longer and longer periods. Every person and every thing seems right to you—that's when you are truly a lover.

How much of a loving person am I? That's really the question.

TANTRIC
DATING
EXERCISES

These Tantric Dating Exercises were specifically designed to help increase our love toward our fellow beings:

1) The Eyes—Your False Friends

We have been conditioned to search for love only from people who look a certain way, dress a certain way, act a certain way, and we go into the dating world looking only for this stereotype. As a practice, first look at people as you usually do. Then, look carefully for attractive characteristics in people you usually dismiss: e.g. that person looks kind, that person looks like they've had a hard day and could use a smile, that person looks like a good provider for their loved ones. See if there is anyone you find sexually attractive even though according to the mainstream conditioning, you aren't supposed to. You can keep this a secret if you like.

2) The Egg Meditation

Designed primarily for women, men can also practice The Egg Meditation to deepen their understanding of yin energy.

3) and 4) Tantric Dating Metta and Tonglen

Traditional Eastern practices for cultivating compassion adapted for Tantric Dating.

5) Practicing Tantric Dating Principles

Questions for your personal reflection to discover your blocks to love.

6) The Perfect Beloved in This Moment

Yes. This one.

EXERCISE #1: The Eyes—Your False Friends

I often send my single patients to Starbucks to sit and people watch, in a different way than they are used to. I ask them to scan for people who look kind, responsible, trustworthy: the type of person, for example, who thinks it would be fun to coach Little League after work. People often get all tangled up in their love lives because the kind of person who would make a good parent to their future kids does not look like the person who fuels their erotic fantasies.

Back when I was studying tantra in India, we did many of our exercises blindfolded. When we couldn't see, we learned to read the information our bodies were giving us about a person, such as whether or not they could be trusted, whether or not their energy was compatible with ours. Experimenting in such an environment of trust and vulnerability, we all fell in love with each other regardless of who our eyes might have prejudged as unworthy.

It seems to me that the way the advertising industry spends billions to convince us that only people who look a certain way are desirable may be related to alarming new statistics about a 60% increase in reports of chronic and crippling loneliness. We are endlessly encouraged to focus on abs and sexiness, not on whether a person would make a good friend or partner. Some of the images selling perfume are downright frightening—if you look closely enough, several of the male models, although conventionally good looking, have the menacing stare of a rapist.

The reports back from Starbucks are that this practice is revolutionary. For many of the clients who come to me lonely and wishing they were partnered, their eyes have become their false friends, encouraging them to search in a way that can't bring them happiness. Osho, the great tantra master, once said, "If you are alone and lonely, it is only because you have too many criteria on your love."

Even if you're not concerned with dating or finding a partner, consider how relying primarily on your eyes for information might be keeping you from more fully exploring smell, touch, sound, and taste. Closing your eyes, getting out of the realm of the visual, is one of the most transformative practices you could take up. In the same way that silence can be the most beautiful sound of all, not seeing in the way you've been trained to see could offer you unexpected vision.

EXERCISE #2: The Egg Meditation

I invented The Egg Meditation after reading *Becoming a Woman* by Dr. Toni Grant. The book was the first time I encountered the idea that as women, we are losing our yin. Dr. Grant never used that language, but as a Jungian she taught that humans are made up of different components or subpersonalities, and that as modern women; we are emphasizing our active "doing" parts at the expense of our quiet "being" parts. Today, women are busy expressing our assertiveness: becoming CEO's, stripping for our lovers and being on top. We reject what has classically been considered female: being quiet, receptive, and demure. We're all yang and no yin.

When I took sex education in high school, we were shown the most amazing video of an egg being impregnated by a sperm. There She sat, unmoving, glowing, queenly, radiating, waiting patiently in all her splendor. The sperm were wriggling and squirming and jockeying for position, all of them anxious to enter Her. One victorious little tadpole finally succeeded. The egg didn't move a muscle, and, except for a little squeal of ecstasy when he entered, appeared unmoved by the whole experience.

The old-fashioned way of pursuit was reportedly like this: men pursued women who were nonactive. Men did all the work. Then during the radical changes of the 70's, Germaine Greer exhorted women to take the lead and pursue whichever men we wanted—it seemed like a good idea at the time. Men and women should certainly do whatever is right for their personal temperament. Nevertheless, neither modern men nor women have any connection to their yin self.

I took some time and meditated on the Egg, imagining myself as Her: sitting silently, radiating, waiting. After practicing a few times, I took it on the road. Since I'm an average looking woman, I'd never been approached all that much in bars, so as usual, I sat and watched all the hotties move on each other. I closed my eyes there on my barstool and did my Egg Meditation, envisioning myself as the Queen Egg, glowing, unmoving, and calm. When I opened my eyes, much to my surprise, several attractive men had wriggled up, jockeying for position. I never got approached so much in all my life as I did that night.

Yang is looking for yin, sorely missing in today's world. I'm not advocating that women give up the gains we've made, not by a long shot. But both men and women are missing the element of yin. That's why some men think they want younger or submissive women. Most modern men don't really want submissive; they want a worthy partner. But yang is looking for yin and not more yang. There has to be a balance.

So just for a few minutes, imagine… you're the queen Egg, sitting unmoving… getting fully in touch with your feminine side.

EXERCISE #3: Tantric Dating
Metta

Metta is a Sanskrit word for friendliness, good will, loving kindness. As a practice it has many forms, many translations. Here is a simple one for you to use to develop and expand your love and kindness toward others:

Lie or sit comfortably with eyes closed. (This prayer can also be said anywhere or anytime as a stealth move, and no one needs to know.) Begin to breathe and repeat the following prayer:

May I be happy.

May I be peaceful

May I be safe.

May I awaken to my true nature.

May I be free.

Think of someone who needs this prayer, someone whom it seems has wronged you, or someone you have trouble loving:

May you be happy.

May you be peaceful

May you be safe.

May you awaken to your true nature.

May you be free.

Then visualize all of us in the world, together:

May all beings be happy.

May all beings be peaceful

May all beings be safe.

May all beings awaken to their true nature.

May all beings be free.

EXERCISE #4: Tantric Dating
Tonglen

Tonglen is a Tibetan Buddhist practice for developing compassion by giving and receiving. The purpose is to reduce selfishness, purify karma, and to develop and expand loving kindness. The Dalai Lama is said to practice *tonglen* daily, and Pema Chodron has written and talked about it.

Start by sitting or lying quietly, and begin to observe the breath. On the next inhale, imagine breathing in the pain of other people, people whose pain is very real to you in some way. This could be an individual you know, one you know of, or a group of people such as refugees or schoolchildren or your family. Breathe in with the longing to relieve their suffering.

Then, when you exhale, send out with your breath to that person or group, comfort and happiness, love and joy. Repeat the inhale and exhale, giving and receiving, until you feel your own heart expanding with love.

Being Tantric Daters, we might imagine breathing in the pain and suffering of all the single people who don't have enough love in their lives, and sending out love and joy and happiness to all.

Osho once said there is nothing wrong with anybody except they didn't get enough love. Let's try in our own small way to rectify that situation.

EXERCISE #5: Practicing Tantric Dating Principles

To put Tantric Dating principles into practice, it's helpful to examine more closely what might be holding us back from love. Using a journal or just sitting quietly, meditate on these questions:

1.   We've been brainwashed into accepting a list of conventional search criteria based on looks, age, financial status, body size, and other unloving prejudices. From a tantric mindset, we might prefer to create a list of loving criteria to guide us. Examples might be: compassionate, kind, shows up in service to others, does some kind of volunteer work, is on a personal growth path. List your original criteria and your new. Which list is more likely to create love in your life?

2.   Consider a time when "chemistry" steered you wrong. What did you learn from this?

3.   Recall a time or a relationship in which you felt rejected, or when you felt you had to reject someone. Is there a way you could reframe that story so nobody, including yourself, got hurt?

4.   If I live in a world in which everyone is evolving, and we're spiritual brothers and sisters helping each other grow, how does that change my mindset when I'm dating? Can I allow other people to be clumsily looking for love, just like I am?

5.   We are all a mixture of yin and yang qualities. Previously it was considered right that men should be yang and women yin, but few of us want to live in that kind of world anymore. What are your yang strengths? How about your yin? What yin qualities have you, perhaps, because we still live in a primarily patriarchal world, judged harshly in yourself or others?

6.   Sit, relax, and breathe, and turn your atten-

tion inward. Where are you holding tension right now? Without trying to change it, notice and become aware—is there often tension in this place? Is it chronic, or just of this moment? Does the attention and breath soften it at all? How is this interfering with being able to experience more pleasure? Exhale and let go…

7.   How could I be a more loving person?

EXERCISE #6: The Perfect Beloved in This Moment

You've heard it many times: truth is in the present moment. The past is made up of memories which are not always accurate as you may have experienced, and the future hasn't happened yet so is all conjecture. Sandwiched in between stands the present moment as the only reality.

I had an overwhelming experience of this sitting quietly at the Burning Ghats, the place where Indians burn their dead. I liked to go sit there and gaze out at the river with the cows, cowherds, and women washing colorful fabrics on the banks. The sun was shining overhead with only a few clouds, the sounds of life murmuring far away from this temple of death, the air rich and pungent as it is in India. Suddenly an awareness shot up my spine ALL IS PERFECT EXACTLY AS IT IS. It filled my body with a streaming vibration for I-don't-know-how-long—an actual tangible experience, not something I read in a book or idle thoughts of the mind. My life changed forever.

If it's true that everything's perfect in the present moment, LOVE must be here too. If I'm not aware of it my mind and my prejudices are keeping me from knowing. If the present moment is perfect, any person I am with is the Perfect Beloved in this moment. Not necessarily in the next moment, or a month or year from now, but who knows?

Practice seeing whomever you are with in this moment as your Perfect Beloved. If you are sitting at the Coffee Bean and a 50-year old man is sitting next to you, practice saying silently to yourself, "This is my perfect beloved in this moment." If you are receiving a massage and enjoying the stranger's hands caressing your body, say to yourself, "This is my lover in this moment." If you are on a date and are not feeling attracted, (you don't have to be to do this exercise) say to yourself, "In this moment, this is where love is. It is up to me in this moment whether I recognize love or not."

Everything is perfect in the present moment.

This person is my Perfect Beloved in this moment.

This is my lover in this moment.

In this moment, this is where love is.

It is up to me in this moment whether I recognize love or not.

Acknowledgments

Thanks to Radha Luglio, Margot Anand, Carolyn Graham Muir, Charles Muir, Sunyata Saraswati, Bodhi Avinasha, Vince Kelvin, Mystery, Prem Prasad, Osho International Meditation Resort, SkyDancing Tantra, Source School of Tantra, Human Awareness Institute, Peter Rengel, and most of all, Osho.

Thanks to Houdini Owens who suggested the book needed to include my story. Thanks for the honest feedback, and for your ongoing journeys in integrity and truth.

Much appreciation to my book designer and editor, Lilly Penhall, for the detailed work and thoughtful suggestions. Thank you for caring about my work.

And of course to my husband, Greg Lawrence, who wanted to date me even after reading this book. Our meeting has taught me that it really is possible for all one's dreams to come true, if you are willing to work for them. Together we embody what comes after Tantric Dating: the creation of a perfect Tantric Soulmate relationship.

Note: I would have liked to thank more women teachers but have found that most female dating coaches and writers inadvertently perpetuate the conventional mindset that women are potential victims of men in the love realms, and that if women become sexual we "lose" something. My experience talking with friends, clients, and spiritual brothers is that men get hurt by love and relationships as much as women do, and that we don't need to protect ourselves from them, or from sex.

About the Author

Catherine Auman, LMFT (Licensed Marriage and Family Therapist) is a spiritual psychotherapist and the Director of The Transpersonal Center. She has advanced training in traditional psychology as well as the wisdom traditions. Catherine lived for a year at the Osho ashram in India—a full-time immersion in tantra and meditation—and she has studied and practiced tantra, love, sex, intimacy, and seduction with numerous teachers. She lives in Los Angeles with her husband, Greg Lawrence, with whom she teaches tantra and relationship enhancement.

Connect with Catherine Auman

Websites:	catherineauman.com
	thetranspersonalcenter.com
Facebook:	catherineaumanlmft
Instagram:	@catherineauman
Youtube:	catherineauman
Eventbrite:	thetranspersonalcenter

Create the Sex, Love and Romance of Your Dreams with *The Tantric Mastery Series*

Tantric Dating

Bringing Love and Awareness to the Dating Process

Catherine Auman, LMFT

Tantric Mating

Using Tantric Secrets to Create a Relationship Full of Sex, Love and Romance

Catherine Auman, LMFT

Tantric Relating

Relationship Advice to Find and Keep Sex, Love and Romance

Catherine Auman, LMFT

Imagine yourself in a perfect soulmate relationship full of sex, love and romance. Open yourself to love and awareness.

These three beautiful books teach you how.

- *Tantric Dating*
- *Tantric Mating*
- *Tantric Relating*

Buy Now online or at your favorite retailer

Print, Ebook, or Audiobook

Works by Catherine Auman

Books

Tantric Mastery Series

> *Tantric Relating: Relationship Advice to Find and Keep Sex, Love and Romance*

> *Tantric Mating: Using Tantric Secrets to Create a Relationship Full of Sex, Love, and Romance*

> *Tantric Dating: Bringing Love and Awareness to the Dating Process*

Mindful Dating: Bringing Loving Kindness to the Dating Process

Guide to Spiritual L.A.: The Irreverent, the Awake, and the True

Shortcuts to Mindfulness: 100 Ways to Personal and Spiritual Growth

Fill Your Practice with Managed Care

Workshops

Tantra: The Science of Creating Your Soulmate

Tantra: The Foundations of Conscious Touch

Tantric Secrets about Women

Tantric Secrets about Men

Tantra and the Psychedelics of Sex

MDMA and Couples Therapy

Audio Recordings

Tantric Embodiment Induction

Deeply Relaxed

Awareness Breathing

Made in the USA
Las Vegas, NV
25 August 2022

53923641R10066